JO

MW01265231

# WATCH

# ME

# DISAPPEAR

HOW TO STAY ANONYMOUS ONLINE,
PROTECT YOUR FAMILY & PRIVACY, OR
DISAPPEAR COMPLETELY

ISBN: 9781080820474

# TABLE OF CONTENTS

---◎---

# INTRODUCTION

Welcome to **Watch Me Disappear**!

I wrote this book with very simple objectives – show you how you can protect your/your family anonymity in the modern world or potentially even disappear off of the face of the planet. No, you will not literally become invisible, but according to every possible piece of tracking information, you will be.

Not everyone understands the necessity to become invisible in the modern world, especially one where everyone is so (happily) plugged into massive tracking systems like *Facebook*, *Google*, or standard banking systems. That being said, there are certain situations where an individual would need to go either partially or completely invisible from the world around them to avoid being found from anyone who may be trying to find them for any reason. Sometimes, disappearing is absolutely necessary to preserve your safety and ensure that you and your family are completely protected from dangers that may lurk in your life.

For me, my need to go invisible was based on my need to protect my family. As a child, I was placed under a mandatory adoption order by the government due to having been born to drug-addicted parents who had physically abused me from the day that I was born. After being raised by my adoptive family, with no contact with my original parents (i.e. a closed adoption arrangement), I had no desire to contact my biological parents whatsoever. They never tried to get in contact with me as well. However things changed when I struck out a few lucky deals in the stock markets in my early twenties. Somehow, my biological father found out about my stock market success and almost immediately began trying to contact me. Quite expectedly, his idea was to get closer to me and my money.

Unfortunately, no matter what I tried, he never stopped stalking me and other members of my adoptive family. Naturally, any sane person would realize that I had zero connection with my biological father and, therefore, blood-related or not, I owed him nothing. However, he seemed to be willing to try anything to attempt to take a stake of my growing wealth. Honestly, I was terrified for my safety and for the safety of my soon-to-be fiancée.

When we discovered that my fiancée was pregnant, I knew that I could no longer take the risk with my biological father. While it was easy enough for me to protect my fiancée from him, the idea of my pregnant fiancée and I enduring that much stress while we were trying to enjoy the reality of our growing family was too much. I *needed* to go under the radar so that my biological father could no longer find us, and my future child would be safe from any threats or potential attacks. That is how I started to research the subject of privacy and learned what is required to go *under the radar*.

Now, truth be told, I have only needed to go under the radar *partially*, because I knew that my paternal father was not wise enough to be able to track me beyond certain more public appearances. However, in the course of my research I met people who were in much more difficult situations and were trying to get *completely* under the radar. Some tried to protect themselves and their families from dangerous involvements with criminals, and others wanted to protect themselves and their children from the dangers of abusive internet stalkers who were trying to harm them. These acquaintances changed the way how I felt about privacy and anonymity on the whole. That's why I have taken this book a step farther and decided to share with you not only my personal experience, but also the experience of people whom I met on my way. My goal is to make sure that you have **the required knowledge to effectively protect yourself and your family from anyone who may be trying to harm you.**

Now, my last point before we move forward – this book is not designed as *complete technical guide* to master all those strategies which I will be describing in the forthcoming pages. The exact technicalities depend too much on specific software and hardware which you use. Moreover, the technology evolves constantly, therefore books which tend to focus on specific software or hardware lose their applicability quickly. However I did my best to capture all those *strategic and tactical steps* which you have to take into account to protect your anonymity. These steps are time proven and unlikely going to change soon.

Enjoy the book and stay safe!

John Forsay

*(as you might have guessed by now, this is my alias)*

# CHAPTER 1

## ANONYMITY

Achieving anonymity is important if you want to protect yourself and your family against the various dangers that could pose a threat to you in the world. When it comes to *disappearing*, however, anonymity is at the core of everything that you want to accomplish, since being anonymous is the primary requirement if you wish to "disappear". Anonymity can occur in varying degrees, depending on just *how well protected* you need to be in order to avoid the dangers that may lurk in your unique circumstances.

In general, I believe that everyone should be practicing at least *some* degree of anonymity to protect themselves from the dangers that we are all naturally exposed to. In a highly plugged-in society, we are at greater risk of being targeted by identity thefts, sexual predators, and other psychopaths or sociopaths who may want to do cruel things to us or our families. I do realize that it may seem like paranoia to some, but the reality is that far too many people have recognized and faced the dangers of living in a plugged-in society, and to those who have experienced those dangers, they would agree that *fully exposing yourself is <u>never</u> a good idea*. Even if you genuinely believe that you are safe from danger, it can strike from the most unexpected places, at the most unexpected times, and leave you wishing that you had done more to protect yourself and/or your family against these dangers.

# DIFFERENT DEGREES OF ANONYMITY

Now, let's start with some basics. Achieving anonymity will require different strategies and tactics, depending on what it is that you are trying to achieve in your life. If you are trying to simply protect yourself from basic dangers, you may not need as much protection as a person who is actively being stalked or harassed by a predator. For example, someone who is in witness protection would need significantly more protection than someone who is simply trying to generally protect themselves by minimizing their exposure to worldly dangers.

The level of anonymity that you need to maintain will depend on the level of protection that you require or are trying to achieve by disappearing. In general, there are three different degrees of anonymity that a person needs to consider: **basic anonymity, intermediate,** or **advanced levels of anonymity**.

For *basic anonymity*, a person will seek to protect themselves from the dangers of the general public by remaining anonymous online and in public places.

For *intermediate anonymity*, a person may be attempting to achieve anonymity from the public, as well as from certain people in their personal network, such as I was.

In *advanced anonymity*, a person is trying to completely hide from everyone. This degree of anonymity is typically only required if a person is under serious threat of being attacked by the people who are searching for them and if they are not able to be adequately protected by those around them.

Believe it or not, each degree of anonymity also comes with its own inherent risks or dangers to a person. Typically, these symptoms or risks increase with the increasing level of anonymity that is required in order to protect a person. Some of these symptoms include mental health risks associated with having to hide or fear for one's safety, increased feelings of isolation or loneliness, potential legal challenges if anonymity is not pursued correctly, or the unfortunate circumstance of anonymity failing to work.

# The Dangers of Becoming Too Exposed

I don't think I need to convince you that there are many potential dangers that people can endure if they are *overly exposed* in the world, whether that is online or offline. These dangers increase depending on how much your general safety is already at risk by those around you. So, for example, if you already have someone who is attempting to find you and harm you, being exposed would be far more dangerous than someone who is not actively being pursued by a predator.

Alternatively, celebrities, people with known wealth, politicians, and other famous people are at a higher risk for becoming targeted by those around them, which can result in these individuals needing to be extra cautious with their level of exposure.

The biggest threat in your level of exposure is having people know *where you are*, which obviously puts you at risk of dangers. For the average person, having people know where you are can make it easy to track you and monitor your daily activities. Individuals or families who are more exposed tend to produce an *"easy in"* for predators, which means that these individuals are at higher risk of becoming targets for predators who may be seeking to kidnap children, commit break and entering's or robberies, steal their identity, or anything else harmful. This means that if it is easy for someone to see *where you are going* and *what you are doing on a regular basis*, a predator could track your routine, follow you, wait for a moment where you are at the right degree of exposure with minimal protection, and then commit their crime. It's likely that you would not expect it to happen, since most people being attacked in this way do not. Thus, you will have no way to protect yourself or your family against this predator which will make you even more vulnerable and exposed to their attack.

For people who are *already vulnerable*, exposure can be the difference between *found and attacked* or staying *hidden and protected*. For example, celebrities will rarely disclose their location online unless they are doing a planned event which will have adequate protection, security, and law enforcement on site to ensure that they and their fans are protected from any potential predators. Likewise, individuals under low-risk witness protection will not share their location or any sensitive information about themselves, their families, or their whereabouts online as this may leave them open to an attack from their potential predators.

Beyond public figures and those under low-risk protection, there are other individuals who need to completely eliminate any exposure they may have to avoid being caught by a persistent predator. For example, individuals under *high-risk witness protection* or those who are *being pursued* and *cannot reasonably seek support from law enforcement* for fear of being exposed by the justice system itself, cannot risk exposing themselves at all. These individuals must eliminate all areas of exposure by disappearing from the online world, changing their name, covering their tracks through the banking system and the legal system, and otherwise cutting off all exposure to the outside world. This does not mean that these individuals will have to go live in the forest or live completely off of the map, but it does mean that these individuals will need to hide any tracks that may lead to them to avoid being caught in a dangerous or even fatal situation.

## How to Achieve Partial Anonymity

Achieving *partial or basic anonymity* is fairly simple. As you will learn about in _Chapter 2_, the biggest key here is to avoid sharing sensitive information online or offline so that people are not able to learn enough about you to turn you into their target. In this situation, you want to avoid sharing your whereabouts, your schedule, or other sensitive information that could lead to you being identified out in public with anyone other than those who you know and trust. For example, you would not want to post *"off to work!"* or *"heading home!"* on your Facebook status every single day, as this could lead to unwanted people learning about your work schedule and then being able to target your home or family for a criminal attack. You also would not want to post your license plate, address (be it text or a picture), phone number, or any information relating to your banking or personal identification online to avoid being stalked or attacked by those who can cause serious harm in your life. In addition to not sharing your own personal information, you want to ensure that your family also does not share personal information to refrain from having anything dangerous happen to them, as well.

# How to Achieve Near-Complete Anonymity

Achieving *near-complete anonymity* will require you to go an extra layer deeper, to ensure that if anyone is trying to find you, they no longer have the capacity to. In this situation, the person trying to find you may be attempting to do harm to you or your family, but they are likely *not motivated enough* to really put the work in to find you if you cover your tracks and become anonymous. For example, when I moved my family into a new city, removed our identifiable stickers from our vehicles, got new license plates, changed our phone numbers, and changed our social media contact information, my paternal father was no longer able to find me. Plus, I knew that he was not motivated enough to hire a PI or anyone else to attempt to find me and continue attempting to threaten us for my money, so I knew that I did not need to do any more than this.

When it comes to achieving near-complete anonymity, you do not need to completely go under the radar but you do need to stop people from being able to find you unless you want them to find you. Typically, your family and friends will need to be on board with this anonymity as well to avoid having someone close to you leaking personal information to those who are attempting to harm you. If your family or friends are not on board, the harsh reality is that you may need to achieve anonymity from them as well to avoid having anyone putting you and your family at risk of being exposed to dangerous people.

# How to Achieve Complete Anonymity

Achieving *complete anonymity* is a life changing decision. The few people I met, who made this decision, went to great lengths to ensure that it was impossible to locate them. In all those cases, they were convinced that it was extremely dangerous if not fatal to them or their families to be located. These individuals had to change their legal names, minimize their involvement in conventional banking systems, move into a new city, change their appearance, cut all ties from virtually everyone that they know, and completely disappear.

It goes without saying that if you decide to completely disappear you will not use social media or online banking or anything else that could connect you to a location service through the internet to avoid being located by persistent predators. Many things will need to be changed to ensure that *every single possible track*, even the one that you would believe to be *"protected"* or *"secure"* such as banking information or legal contracts, are hidden completely. For such individuals, any level of exposure can be extremely dangerous, so they are not exposed at all. Consider the creator of Bitcoin for example

— no one knows who created this wildly successful technology and no one would be able to find out even if they wanted to because they would be unable to identify who exactly created the system. Although many people have ideas as to who the company was established by and there is a head figure (*Satoshi Nakamoto*) who is often portrayed as the creator, no one truly knows. This is the result of having complete anonymity.

# CHAPTER 2

## GENERAL PRIVACY FOR YOURSELF AND YOUR FAMILY

C reating general privacy for yourself and your family is not too challenging and it comes with very few (if any) risks to mental health in terms of producing feelings of isolation or fear of predators. When you create general privacy for yourself and your family, your goal is not to achieve complete anonymity but instead simply to minimize your exposure to the outside world in order to avoid becoming the target for a potential predator. Here, you want to make sure that you are not being too open and making it easy for someone to successfully plot and execute a devastating attack on you or your family.

There are two areas where you are going to want to protect yourself and your family when it comes to creating general privacy: *online* and *offline in the general public*. Let's proceed with learning what it means exactly to generate this level of privacy for yourself and your family.

## WHAT CONSTITUTES AS BASIC LEVELS OF PRIVACY

Basic privacy for you and your family does not mean that you are *never* seen or that you can *never* share information about your family with others. When it comes to basic privacy, you are simply *being cautious* about the type of information that you are sharing with those around you, including both intentional and unintentional messages that you share. You may call it an "*anonymity hygiene*", if you wish – and I believe this is the minimum requirement for any person and especially for people with families in the modern world.

*Online, basic privacy* means that you are not sharing sensitive information in areas where it could be used to harm you. At this point you're probably thinking: "*wait, but isn't it a bit too general - in theory anything can be used in a harmful way*". Yes and no. Since we're talking about the basic level of privacy, I assume that you don't have a "*professional*" criminal trying to get to you or your family. Thus, your goal is simply to create a *virtual wall* around yourself and your family to avoid any unwanted risks.

What this means in reality is that you shouldn't allow any of the following information to become publically available on the internet:

- *Current and potential whereabouts* (home address, school address, job address, your schedule, vacation plans etc),
- *Personal identifiable information* (license plate information, your full legal name, your birth date and the birth date of your children or other family members, information associated with legal identification documents etc),
- *Sensitive information about your social status / financial details* (income level, your banking information – credits, savings etc),

*- Anything else that could expose the details about your private life* (your relatives, former relationships, friends and colleagues, intimate life etc).

Sharing such personal information online, **even just once**, can result in people discovering just the right amount of information for them to plan an attack on your family.

Now, when it comes to *offline privacy*, the idea is that you should limit the exposure of the same types of information as I listed for online privacy. However in the offline world, realistically, it's *much easier* to avoid parading this type of information. And most of us were raised to be cautious in public. So simply avoid *openly* and *loudly* discussing such things as your home or job addresses, your schedule or vacation plans or any other personal identification information.

Make sure that you are not putting out *accidental information*, such as by using those stick people figures that you place on your car which tell others how many people are in your car and what age they are. Most of the time, basic offline privacy is simply ensured by *eliminating accidental leaks* of information. This way you can ensure that no one has the capacity to identify who you are, easily recognize your vehicle in a public place, and begin tracking you so that you can become their next target.

# ACHIEVING BASIC PRIVACY ONLINE

Let's talk now about the specifics of achieving basic level of online privacy. The rules are quite simple to follow and mostly relate to *social media*:

- Be cautious about what you share in your status on social media,
- Use stricter privacy settings on ALL of your social media platforms,
- Do not add anyone you do not know as "friends",
- Use only secured online banking features.

As well, one more general rule here (as it's impossible to foresee all potential situations) - ***never ever exchange personal information through the internet***. If a friend needs information such as your address, simply call them and provide them with that information through the telephone. If you are doing business through email and a company needs access to a photocopy of your driver's license, have that company call you and arrange to transfer that information in a different way. *Never put sensitive information online*, even if it seems harmless, as this can become dangerous to you or anyone else who is connected with you.

Now, a few important words about setting your *family security standards on social media*. I encourage you to have a separate conversation about this with all your family members. No matter how shocking it may sound, this conversation is a very important first step in ensuring your online safety. The main idea that you would want everyone to follow – *"we have to become very strict about what is allowed to reveal yourself and our family on the internet in general and social media specifically"*. Everyone in your family has to follow the rules which I outlined above. Your family needs to know that anyone who *is not someone you know in real life cannot become a part of your "family circle"*. It's especially important if you have kids – in spite of this modern craze of collecting "likes" for everything they do, they have to refrain from becoming "friends" with those, whom they don't know in real life (and that means not adding them as "friends" on social media).

Of course, you have to do some basic adjustments in your *social media privacy settings*. Make sure that you set your privacy settings to the "maximum" level to ensure that anyone attempting to see your profile who does not actively have you added is unable to see anything aside from your profile picture and your name (since these cannot be hidden from others.) As well, make sure that the pieces of information that can be seen publicly do not make it easy for you to be identified so that you are not found by anyone whom you do not want to be found by.

One last word about the general online privacy. It's important to always keep in mind that any information placed on the internet can be accessed by *anyone who wants to*, even if your privacy settings are strict. There are codes that people can type into social media platforms to gain access to any profile they want, there are back doors and ways to collect information through scraping and parsing methods. And I'm not even talking about the intended and unintended leaks from such major companies as Google or Facebook, who spend literally hundreds of millions on their security. Here you may read more about it:

- https://techcrunch.com/2019/07/11/google-is-investigating-the-source-of-voice-data-leak-plans-to-update-its-privacy-policies
- https://www.cnbc.com/2018/10/08/google-bug-exposed-the-information-of-up-to-500000-users.html
- https://www.theverge.com/2018/12/14/18140771/facebook-photo-exposure-leak-bug-millions-users-disclosed

So make sure that you are still being cautious about what you share online *even* if your privacy settings are strict. Although the average person may not know these advanced technical tools, predators and attackers of all sorts can gain this information from the black market and use it to target unexpecting people.

# ACHIEVING BASIC PRIVACY OFFLINE

Let's talk about the specific steps of achieving basic level of *offline privacy*. As I mentioned earlier, ensuring your offline privacy is more natural for us as we were raised as being more cautious in the *real world*. Therefore, the most important first step towards achieving basic offline privacy is about *minimizing accidental information leaks*. Offline, you want to make sure that any visible identification features are not actively being displayed for people to see, such as the car stickers mentioned previously.

That said, there are also many similar things that people do which automatically put their family at risk of being exposed to the public. The irony is that a lot of these things are even *considered to be helping to protect our families,* but in reality can actually be incredibly dangerous. A common example of this innocent but dangerous exposure would be writing your *child's name, phone number, and address on their backpack* so that if they are lost or if the backpack is lost, it can be returned. The intention behind this may be positive or innocent, but the reality is that you have just given a potential predator all of the information they need to locate your child. Unfortunately, even the parents in the school where your child attends should not be considered as safe since predators can lurk anywhere, and not surprisingly, tend to hang out in the vicinity of those who they want to harm.

You also want to make sure that you are cautious about the *information that you are carrying with you and showing to others.* For example, refrain from carrying your social security number, your birth certificate, your passport, or any other identification documents with you unless you actually need to use those pieces of information on that particular outing. Otherwise, leave everything at home so that it is not accidentally lost and then potentially found by someone who could do something incredibly dangerous or harmful with it. Typically, carrying your driver's license is all you need.

Also be cautious about the information that you are sharing with people and *the volume that you are speaking in.* You never know if people might be listening, so if you begin speaking too loudly while sharing personal information, you may put yourself and your family at risk. If you are sharing your address with the dentist receptionist, for example, speak quietly and ensure that no one is listening or paying close attention to what you are saying. Always ensure that you stay aware of your surroundings and if you feel like something is strange or someone seems to be following you or paying closer attention to you than what you feel is normal, make sure that you stay alert. While you do not need to become paranoid, staying alert and watching over your shoulder can ensure that you are not being put at unnecessary risk of becoming a target.

# Basic Protection for Children

I have already mentioned a few important safety rules when it comes to children. Unfortunately, children have a tendency to be the most vulnerable when it comes to attacks that are being made on unsuspecting people, likely because children are the easiest part of the population to target. Since children are not yet experienced with the world around them, and in many cases, are not yet old enough to comprehend the dangers of predators, many are unaware of what it takes to stay safe from harm. Beyond their intellect around potential dangers, children are also less capable of protecting themselves physically since most attackers can easily overpower the child and leave them unable to prevent the attack from happening.

The biggest risk to children is sexual predators, including people who want to sexually take advantage of them and people who want to kidnap them to put them in front of sexual predators. The children's sex trade is unfortunately a very real, massive, and global danger that children from all over the world are at risk of being kidnapped and put into against their will, and with very few ways of tracking them down once they

33

are gone. Hopefully, I don't need to do a lot more convincing here, so I will mention just a few facts for you. According to the estimates of The International Labor Organization, forced labor and human trafficking is a booming $150 billion industry worldwide. Among the victims of this "industry" 25% are children. In the US, it is estimated that 1 out of 7 endangered runawas (who were reported to the National Center of Missing and Exploited Children) were likely child sex trafficking victims.

Aside from sexual predators, there are also predators who are clinical psychopaths or sociopaths that will do cruel things to children for their own twisted pleasures. In our modern world, there is an additional risk being posed to children: bullies who are able to target the child from the internet and follow them into real life to begin physically attacking and harming the child. Internet bullying has led to suicide, physical attacks, and alienation from their peers in many children's lives, which makes it an incredibly dangerous form of attack that can be taken on children.

While some parents prefer to withhold from their children any information which can lead them to feeling unsafe, I believe the opposite should be done. The best way to protect your children is to *educate them on the dangers of the world around them* - in a way that they are able to understand based on their age. Ensure that from the moment they start school, if not sooner, your child knows how to identify things like appropriate and inappropriate touching, people who are prying for too much information, or people who are following them. Teach your children that if they ever feel unsafe or are approached by someone dangerous, they need to contact a trusted adult *right away* and let that adult know everything, even if they are afraid or ashamed of the information that they are sharing.

You also need to make sure that your child is not being exposed excessively by ensuring that they are *not using the internet in any dangerous way*. Ensure that your child uses age-appropriate platforms only (beware of *TikTok* and similar 'children/teen targeted' platforms) and that they use these platforms in a way that protects their privacy and their general safety. Teach your child never to add anyone that they do not know, never to share sensitive information with anyone including people they do know, and never to post things online that can exploit them or expose them in a way that is dangerous or harmful to their safety. Again, if your child does feel like something inappropriate is happening online or with their internet experience, make sure that they are taught to come to you and share that information right away to avoid putting themselves at unnecessary risk.

You also need to make sure that you keep an eye on your child and that you are *proactive with their protection*. When you are in public, do not let them venture too far away until they are old enough to reasonably manage their own protection in the area that you are in. For example, you would not want to let your five-year-old walk around the mall alone, but you may let your fourteen-year-old walk around on their own while you are in the same mall as they are. You can never be too cautious when it comes to looking out for your child's protection, so do not be afraid to hold their hand, risk looking disinterested in a friendly conversation in favor of watching your child play on the playground, or refuse them walking around on their own. The more you are involved in their protection, the more you can minimize their risk of exposure to the world around them since your child does not yet know how to do that for themselves.

Lastly, make sure that your child understands that *you are a safe person for them to turn to and that they can trust you*. Many times, children who are at risk or who have been exposed to a predator will fear turning to their parents because they believe that their parents will not understand, or that they will be angry with them for what has happened. When a child is at risk or has been approached by a predator, the predator will often engage in a behavior known as *"grooming"*, where they groom the child to trust them and feel safe in their presence. Then, because the child trusts this person, they are less likely to say anything to anyone because they have been *groomed* to stay quiet and do as the predator has asked. This can result in your child willingly engaging in dangerous behaviors with dangerous people because they have come to trust that the other person has their best interest at heart, even if they do not. This is a common behavior from predators, so you need to openly teach your child to look out for it and ensure that they trust you deeply as well, so that, should anyone try anything inappropriate with them, they know that they can turn to you for help and that you will help protect them.

## WHAT TO DO IF YOU FEEL TARGETED

Now, let's imagine a hypothetical situation. Let's assume that you are being targeted by someone – for instance, you see someone following you or feel as though someone is prying for more information than what seems reasonable for that person. What to do in this case?

First off, make sure you take the *basic protection steps* which we discussed earlier. Secondly, if you have this individual on your social media profiles, *immediately delete these profiles and ensure that your family deletes them as well* so that this person cannot simply find information from a different source. Should you believe that you are being followed, gain as much information about this person as you can and then *call the local authorities to report the individual*. Please, do not follow *"let's wait and see"* logic. The earlier you involve your local authorities – the better. Even though you may not be able to press charges to get protection from law enforcement right away, if anything does happen, they have information on hand that proves you have been dealing with this individual for a while. In other words, they can begin to build a case against this individual which means that they are more likely to get their due justice should they actually try to do anything to you or your family.

In addition to alerting local authorities, make sure that your family and loved ones know exactly *who to look out for, so that they can protect themselves*. Have the discussion with your children and loved ones and make sure that they are aware of how to protect themselves and what to do in case of a threatened attack so that they can stay safe from a potential predator.

In most cases, as long as a predator realizes they have been caught and you are on to them, they will stop attempting to target you and they will move on to find someone else who is vulnerable or exposed. However, you should not rely on this as the minute you let your guard down, you go back to becoming overexposed and vulnerable to the predator again.

Since the predator already has information accumulated on you and your family, increasing your exposure can make it easy for them to come back and attempt their attack once again when you are not expecting it. In fact, *many predators will use this as a tactic to try and get your guard down before attacking.* So be cautious and realize that once you are on someone's radar, it can be very difficult for you to completely protect yourself once again without staying alert at all times.

# CHAPTER 3

---

## GOING PARTIALLY UNDER THE RADAR

Going partially under the radar is sometimes necessary if you need to protect yourself from certain people who seem to be negatively impacting your safety or the safety of your family. If you are worried about a family member or a friend, for example, you may need to go partially under the radar and protect yourself against this individual. Alternatively, if you suspect that you are being followed or targeted by someone, you may also decide to go partially under the radar to prevent you from becoming a target who has actually been attacked by the predator in question.

Going partially under the radar requires you to increase your confidentiality, further decrease your online presence, and be more cautious about who you spend time with and where you spend your time.

How you will achieve your partial disappearance will ultimately depend on where you believe your highest risk of exposure exists and what you need to do in order to protect yourself from that risk of exposure. That being said, do not be so naive as to believe that if you are exposed, it *only exists in one place*: people who may be attempting to track you will want to have the *"insurance"* of having information on you in many different areas. Just because someone has found you online and has only made advances through social media, for example, does not mean that they have not found information about your *offline life* so that they can track you in the real world should you block them from the internet. Likewise, a person who has been following you *offline* will likely have found you *on the internet* so that they can track you and your family online as well and increase the amount of information that they gain from you.

Needing to go partially under the radar in one area of your life will always require an increased level of attentiveness and protection in other areas of your life as well to avoid being exposed to additional dangers or threats. Remember, those who are naive or who put their guard down are the ones who become instantly at risk of becoming attacked, so you always need to be on guard to a degree when it comes to protecting yourself and your family from potential attackers.

# How Challenging Will it be to Track You Down

When it comes to *partial anonymity* to the point of going *partially under the radar*, tracking you down becomes a lot more challenging because you have buried most of your tracks. For the average public, finding you will be nearly impossible because you have hidden from the public eye. For people who *want to find you*, however, it will still be possible as there will still be legal tracks that lead to where you are. For example, the FBI or a highly motivated predator could easily hire a PI to track some of your personal information and find you, which means that if you are highly at risk of a very lucrative predator, you need to go much further than a partial disappearance. However, if your fear is simply being found by a family member that you want nothing to do with (like it was in my case), you can be confident that a partial disappearance is plenty to keep you protected from anyone who may be trying to find you.

# Steps and Techniques to Achieve Partial Disappearance

The following steps are tools that you can use to effectively go under the radar to avoid being found by anyone who might be looking for you. I will reiterate that these strategies will not *completely* protect you from anyone who may be trying to look for you, but they will protect you from the average person.

### *Email, Social Media, and the Internet*

Email, social media, and the internet, in general, can be a fairly dangerous place for anyone, but especially someone who is trying to protect themselves or their families from potential threats to their safety. The universal internet transparency principle applies - *once something is on the internet, it is on there forever*. So you need to make sure that you and your family are using the internet properly to avoid being put at risk by a dangerous predator.

## Cautious Usage

We have spent enough time discussing the need for *cautious internet usage* in the *basic privacy* part of the book. And while it may seem redundant to repeat the same principle here, this is a crucial first step. With the latest technological advancements it's impossible to predict what kind of online services are going to be invented in the years to come. Thus, you have to rely on your judgement which internet services may be potentially harmful. So the first step to ensuring that you are protected on the internet is to use *predictive thinking* – always keep in mind *how* you are using the internet and *what* you are using it for.

Of course, it goes without saying that you need to refrain from sharing any information through emails, social media sharing sites, or messengers as information on these platforms can easily be hacked into and stolen by anyone who is interested in finding that information. So, wherever possible, use 2-factor authentication for your accounts, change your passwords regularly and never use simplistic phrases, names, geographical locations and numbers in your passwords (more on that later).

Since we're describing a more dangerous situation here, you cannot exclude that you won't be dealing with hackers. They can use multiple tricks to get the needed information. For instance *brute force* your personal and family accounts – i.e. by simply trying readily available databases of logins/passwords with the hope of eventually finding the right combination. If they succeed, they will get into your profile and copy anything that they want to know, which is listed in your profile/your mailbox. If someone is trying to target you for something, such as *identity theft* or *burglary*, hacking your accounts is typically the first step for them to get access to your information. Be aware of this if you suspect that someone is after you or your family.

*Passwords and Protective Features: a few special words*

Most modern social media platforms and other internet platforms have a greater level of security than they used to. While this increased security cannot completely protect you from hackers, it can mitigate your risk of being hacked, so it is valuable to take advantage of these security features for your online platforms. One additional security step when it comes to your passwords is to start using a *password manager* that will propose unique complicated passwords for each social media/mail account which you have (Dashlane, LastPass, 1Password or similar). The proposed passwords will contain a mixture of letters, numbers, and symbols, and that they will be different on every single platform, so that if someone hacks into one of your accounts, they cannot hack into all of them.

When it comes to "2-factor authentication" - these systems require you to log in using your password and then verify that it is you attempting to log in by providing a code that was sent to either your email address or your cell phone. Unless the individual attempting to hack you has access to your email or your cell phone, they will not be able to get into your account which means that your account will be safe.

Of course, certain high tech hackers may be able to get through even the safest of systems, but these hackers are typically not a major risk to the average person as they are in search of "higher quality" information in their pursuits. Unless you are storing sensitive information on your social media accounts or you have a high amount of money at risk, you are likely not going to be impacted by these individuals. That being said, you still need to be cautious just in case you do become under attack from an individual like this, so do not let your guard down even if you believe that you are safe.

*Photographs and Updates*

What you post on social media or on any internet-based platform needs to be carefully screened to ensure that you are not uploading anything that could give away sensitive information to those who are paying attention. This means that in addition to platforms like Facebook and Twitter, you also need to be cautious with your email and any cloud-based backup services that you may be using to store your sensitive information on. If you are trying to protect yourself from being identified, *never upload anything that shares your face or the faces of your family* so that those who may find your social media accounts cannot identify that they do, in fact, belong to you.

## Laptop Computers and Cell Phones

Laptops and cell phones are connected to the wireless internet, which means that anything they are used for is automatically at a higher risk than anything being shared on wired internet connections or wired phone connections. For that reason, be cautious when using laptops or cell phones for things like online banking or backing up or storing sensitive information, since *they are easier to tap into and hack* than their alternative.

## Location Tracking Services

A hidden landmine that can give you away quickly if you are trying to cover your tracks is the location services on your laptop or your cell phone. Location services can track where your cell phone or computer is which can give away your location as well, making it easy for someone to track you if they wanted to. Be cautious when using apps like Snapchat, as these have built-in geofilters and geomaps which give your audiences direct information about where you are with real-time updates. Another unexpected way that location services can give away your location is those that are connected to your photographs, which can then be uploaded onto social media and identified by someone who may be willing to do the work to look into the picture's information. Even a simple status update can give away your location information if your location services are on, which makes it a very dangerous tool for people who are trying to keep their location hidden. *You should turn off your location services for everything on your phone and laptop* to avoid having your location made known to people through your social media or other internet-based interactions.

## Business and Career

Your place of work can be one of the most challenging areas to keep your life anonymous because most of us cannot afford to simply quit our career and hide away. Unfortunately, you need to continue making money to survive even if you need to hide, so you need to do extra work to ensure that you are staying anonymous through your work life.

*Keeping Your Work Life Separate*

The best way to keep yourself protected at work is to *keep your work life and home life separate.* Do not tell people at work about your private life, even if you think that you are friends as this can leave you vulnerable and exposed. At the end of the day, you do not completely know everyone you work with and you cannot guarantee that you are safe to share information with all of your co-workers and employers. Instead, be very cautious about the information that you share and refrain from sharing anything unnecessary. If private information is needed, such as your address for your employer, make sure that you provide it quietly and in a private area so that not everyone knows where you are from. Do not give information to just anyone if they ask or give vague answers if you can, to avoid having people who may be prying for your personal information.

When it comes to your personal life, do not give too much information about where you work, what your schedule is, or what your route to work is unless you are sharing with someone close to you like your spouse. Be cautious about where this information is made available so that you are not giving people the information that they need to make you their target. For example, do not upload your place of work on social media as this can result in you being targeted by people online. Plus, this information is typically made available in a public way even if your profile is private, which means that once it is on there you cannot take it off or hide it because even if you remove it from your profile, it still exists in the history of your profile. Therefore, if someone were really adamant about finding out about you, they could learn through some basic coding tricks that will reveal any information like that to them within seconds.

## *Home and Address*

Your home can be *one of your most vulnerable places* since people are typically not on guard when they are in their own homes. There will be periods where you are relaxing watching TV, where your kids may be in the yard playing by themselves, or when you may be asleep which can all be times that you are vulnerable. Furthermore, your home itself is at risk anytime you are not home, which means anything that is inside of your home is also at risk. You need to make sure that you only give your address to the people who you trust and that you keep your home protected using proper locks and safety features to avoid having anyone break in or attack when you are vulnerable.

## Rent or Lease, Not Own

If you need increased protection, favoring renting or leasing over owning property can be helpful as the owners of various properties are typically public information. Anyone could easily look up your name in certain real estate databases and locate your information, thus meaning that they instantly get access to your home address. If you rent or lease, however, this information is not put in a public database because the owner of the property will be your landlord, not you. As a result, if anyone were to try and look you up this way, they could not find you.

## Never Give Out Your Address

Anytime you need to meet up with someone or you want to spend time with someone, *avoid giving them your address* as much as possible unless they are someone you really trust. Instead, meet people in public places or at their own home so that you do not have to invite them into your space. People who you do not know well or trust well can easily come into your home and start looking around to gain information about the layout of your house and any safety features that your house may have. Plus, once they know where you live, they can start paying attention to your schedule by quietly stalking your home either by staking out in cars or by getting people they know to walk by and start casing out your property.

If you are someone who does business from your home or who sells things second-hand from your home, always find *secure remote locations to meet up* with people. Instead of having clients come to your home, consider renting a public facility to use where you can meet your clients. These days, there are many small office spaces that you can easily rent so that you can begin meeting clients in a public location. Plus, you can use this public address for your mailing information rather than your home address, which makes it safer for you and your family if you are running a home business with many different clients.

If you are selling something second hand, many police stations or public facilities will offer safe meet up locations so that you can sell your items in public without having to have someone come to your home and purchase it. These arrangements can be more challenging as you have to leave your home to meet up with someone so they take more time and resources, but they ensure that people do not know where you live and are not able to start casing out your property. It is worth the added effort to ensure that you and your family are protected from unexpected predators who may be dangerous to you or your family.

*Public and Private Mailboxes*

When you are trying to go under the radar, having public and private mailboxes is valuable to ensure that people are not able to acquire your mailing address without your permission. The best way to prevent people from getting your address through your mailbox is by renting a mailbox away from your home. Most mailing companies will offer private mailboxes for a fairly inexpensive price. You can rent these mailboxes out, get a unique PO box number, and then have all of your mail sent to that mailbox rather than your personal mailbox at home. That way, should anyone ever attempt to get your address through your personal mail, they will only find themselves at your PO box and not at your home.

## Family and Friends

Unfortunately, if you are trying to stay under the radar, having family and friends who may give information as to where you are to the people whom you are trying to avoid can make all of your efforts worthless. If you want to successfully go partially under the radar, you need to ensure that anyone who you associate with is not going to give your information away and have you found by the very people whom you are trying to stay away from. If you have children, you also need to teach your children not to share private information about your family with their friends, either, as this could result in them accidentally letting people know where you are and how you can be found.

*Informing Family and Friends*

When you inform family and friends about your decision to go partially under the radar, *make sure that you are clear about your intentions,* and if possible, be clear about *how serious* it is that you stay partially hidden. If your family and friends understand how serious your need to stay hidden is, they will be more likely to take it seriously and refrain from telling others about where you are, or any other sensitive information that you need to keep private. When your friends and family are not sure about how serious it is, they are less likely to take you seriously and may tell people about your private information without realizing what they are putting you at risk for.

Of course, there may be situations when you may not be able to disclose all of the information relating to your need to partially disappear to your loved ones. If this is the case, share what you can and keep the rest private. Ask that your family and friends trust you and respect your privacy and that they refrain from telling anyone about important information regarding you and your family. You will need to decide what these parameters are based on how far under the radar you need to go, but typically this should involve things like not disclosing your phone number or address, not sharing your social media accounts or tagging you in posts, and not telling anyone about where you work. You may also request more privacy depending on what you need. Make sure that you are clear about your privacy needs, however, so that those closest to you do not accidentally disclose any information to another individual without your consent.

## Dealing With Those Who Do Not Support You

Sadly, there are situations in life when not everyone in your family is going to fully support you or who do not know how to keep your information private when it comes to going under the radar. In this case, my suggestion is to look at the situation from a cold rational standpoint. You will have to make an important decision — do you value *this person* or *your privacy more*? If you need to stay private no matter what, you may need to be very cautious about what information you share with this family person and ensure that *everyone else in your family circle knows not to share any sensitive information with the individual*, either. This way, you can continue spending time with this person but they will be unable to know anything important enough for them to share. If the person is especially difficult or unwilling to support you in protecting your privacy, unfortunately you will need to consider eliminating them from your close circle or from your life entirely to avoid having them expose you and your family when you are trying to stay protected. I understand that this can be challenging and even heartbreaking, but when it comes to you and your family's protection, it can sometimes be necessary as well.

*A Word about Acquaintances*

Not everyone in your life is going to be a close friend or family member. When it comes to dealing with acquaintances or friends who you are not particularly close with, you do not necessarily have to eliminate them from your life but you are going to need to be more cautious with these individuals. You want to avoid giving them any information that they may be able to share with others, which would then expose you and your family.

The best way to continue to be friends with acquaintances or friends who are not particularly close with you is to refrain from allowing conversations to move toward personal topics. For example, instead of talking about where you work or what community you live in, talk about what your beliefs are or a recent sports game. These types of topics allow you to remain friends with people without making it seem like you are trying to be secretive or hide anything. If the topic of your personal life does come up, avoid sharing anything overly personal and instead only share information that does not go too deep into identifying you or your family. For example, if they ask where you live, instead of saying *"On 4ᵗʰ street by the corner store,"* say *"in the northwest."* This way, you are giving away some information and naturally engaging in the conversation without directly giving away your location or private information.

Another important point about acquaintances – always make sure that *you are aware of who their circle is,* too. These individuals can be somewhat dangerous as they may know the very people that you are trying to stay away from, or they may be closer to those people than you think. Since you are not going to outright ask them if they know the said person or people, your best bet is to simply stay private and reserved in these relationships. That way, you are not accidentally exposing yourself through people who are unaware of the fact that you are trying to stay private and hidden from people.

*Teaching Your Child to Stay Private*

From my own practice, it can be particularly challenging to educate children on how to stay private. This is simply because they tend to not fully understand the importance of staying private when it needs to happen. Furthermore, you may not want to make the idea of having to stay private scary, which could lead to your child having fears around the need to be private.

Instead, the better way to teach your child to stay private is to *disclose as little information as possible* when it comes to informing them about your lives. For example, do not tell your child where you work or where your spouse works, and instead keep that information private. When it comes to teaching your child about your home address, phone number, and other such information, ensure that they are aware that they should only be sharing this information with people who are important and trustworthy. For example, if the principal asks for their phone number, they can disclose it, but if anyone like a friend's parent at school asks, make sure that your child knows to say *"no"*. Instead, say that if they want that information, they can come to you to get it. If your friend wants to connect with their friends after school, teach them to be the one taking down information and then reaching out to their friends so that they are not accidentally giving away private information innocently.

## *Facial Recognition*

When it comes to partially going under the radar or completely going under the radar, one of the most dangerous things you have to concern yourself with is facial recognition. If someone recognizes you or any member of your family, they can easily begin tracking you and then find out important information such as what car you are driving and what house you are living in. The best way to deal with potential facial recognition is to change the look of yourself and your family members as much as possible. If necessary, you might also need to move to a new city or state where no one will be able to recognize you because you are not associated with anyone in the area.

Changes can include wearing your makeup differently, dressing differently, and getting new hairstyles. While hiding children can be more challenging, the benefit is that they often look different as they age so they will already have a different appearance naturally in no time at all. You and your spouse might need to work a little harder, however, such as by wearing clothes or accessories that help hide your identity when you are going out. Hoodies, hats, big sunglasses, and scarves can all help you hide your identity better in public so that no one can identify you and begin tracking you.

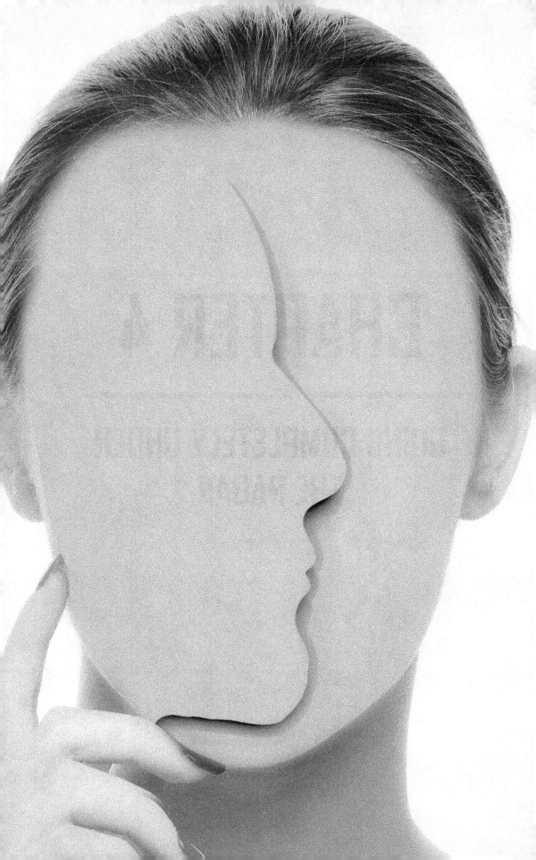

# CHAPTER 4

## GOING COMPLETELY UNDER THE RADAR

I will say this upfront – in this day and age, if you are in a situation where you need to go *completely under the radar*, it is going to be *much more challenging* and will require serious drastic measures in order to protect you from the people who might be trying to cause problems in your life. In this situation, you are going to literally bury *every single trail* that may point toward where you are, which means that you are going to need to get into changing legal names, addresses, banking documents, and anything else which could lead people toward you.

However it is also important to understand that unless you're trying to hide from the government/law enforcement (in this case you will have to search for another book and probably not on Amazon), the key when going completely under the radar is making sure that **you do it legally**. This is crucially important as I've seen a lot of ill-advised articles suggesting various illegal ways of *"disappearance"*. You really need to avoid incriminating situations which could result in you having a much larger problem on your hands.

That is why we are going to explore the steps to take in order to <u>completely</u> and also <u>legally</u> go under the radar so that you cannot be found by anyone. While there is still a slim chance that you can be found, your likelihood of being caught is extremely small if you do this correctly.

# Legally Going Under the Radar

So why is it important to remain within the legal boundaries when attempting to *disappear*? Legally going under the radar means that you cannot just disappear, smuggle yourself across the border into a new country, and start fresh. People who attempt to do this often end up abandoning contractual commitments such as leases, debt payments, and other legal commitments which can lead to incrimination and fraudulent charges. This is not a way to go under the radar, as you can imagine, but a way to get you literally **on the radar**. Stay away from any advice that may lead to bigger troubles! Make sure that you are not evading your legal responsibilities or using *"going under the radar"* as an opportunity to abandon your legally bound commitments so that you can refrain from incriminating yourself and facing potential jail time should you ever get caught.

The reality is such – if you are lucky, going under the radar legally for a few years will be plenty and then you can surface again when the waters are cleared and it is safe for you to do so. If this is your circumstance, you to want to have the capacity to show up and not worry about facing legal charges due to illegal behaviors. However even if this is *not* your circumstance, the government may still be able to locate you which means that if you are caught going under the radar from both your attackers and the government, you may stand to *get caught by your attacker and face significant legal charges in the meantime*. Clearly, this is not a wise choice. Therefore the techniques outlined in this book will support you in going under the radar legally so that you can protect yourself without incriminating yourself.

# UNDERSTANDING YOUR ATTACKERS AND WHAT THEY MIGHT DO

The first step in going under the radar completely relates to something we discussed before – **predictive thinking**. Your initial move should be to *understand your attacker* and what their likely approach is going to be when it comes to *planning their attack on you*.

Every single attacker will behave differently, so universal advises don't work here. You know your situation best of all and that gives you a unique insight as to what can you expect in their attempts to find you and harm you.

➤ For example, an abusive ex-spouse who is attempting to gain access to their children may go through lawyers to try and locate you and make it seem as though you are the bad parent for taking your kids away, rather than them being the bad parent for attacking you. They will likely try and stalk you and locate incriminating information about you so that they can manipulate the lawyers and legal system to work in their favor and put you and your children back in harm's way. In this case, your life may or may not be at risk depending on how abusive your ex-spouse is and what they are likely to achieve. Some may be willing to go to life-threatening risks in their abusive behaviors, whereas others may simply try to play the legal system and force you and your kids back into their life.

➢ Alternatively, if you owe someone shady a lot of money, they likely have the means to locate you and physically harm you or your family in an effort to recuperate their money that you have borrowed from them. You need to do a lot more to protect yourself from angry mobsters or gangsters since you and your family are much more likely to be at risk of actually suffering severe damages or even fatalities if these individuals find you.

The best way to ensure that you are thinking like your attacker is to first consider *what their true motives* are for finding you and *how aggressive* they can actually be.

Let's take an example. Someone who is *mentally aggressive* and who is likely to stick to *manipulation or mind tactics* to attempt to harm you, for example, is less likely to be physically dangerous to you or your family. These individuals are more likely to use smart strategies over brute force, which means that they will likely *take time* to attempt to find you through family members, social media, your place of work, or even your banking statements or telephone records. If they were married to you, chances are they have a much easier opportunity to access this information. In this situation you probably have time to think through your *"disappearance"*. Your best defense strategy for such cases will be *"maximum cautiousness"* about the information that your attacker can access and how you are storing your information with different organizations, companies, on the internet etc. Your second goal would be to ensure that you are *far enough away* – i.e. that you are not likely to be located by this person (or whomever teams up with this person) through facial recognition, which could result in them simply stalking you and finding you.

If your attacker has *more aggressive tendencies*, such as if they are actually potentially going to become a life-threatening risk to you or your family, you need to address your situation with far more caution. In these extreme circumstances, you may not have a lot of time to contemplate. You will have to *disappear quickly* and *far away* to avoid being found by them as these individuals are unlikely to take time to attempt manipulating you or use scare tactics to get to you. Instead, once they find you, they will begin physically abusing you and your family, or worse, and they will likely not waste any time in becoming extremely physically dangerous since they know that their window of opportunity is minimal. For that reason, you need to do everything in your power to make sure that you are absolutely never located by this individual or group of individuals.

I will say it once again. There is no magic trick here - *no one will know your attacker as well as you do*. So you need to honestly assess how likely your attacker is to become aggressive and how motivated they are to find you. You also need to consider what they may try to do in order to gain access to you so that you can bury those trails *before* they have the opportunity to access them. Once the trails are buried, they need to stay buried so that there is no way for you to be located at any point in the future, either.

Lastly, one more point on the strategy before we get to specific tactics. The minute you choose to disappear and you start making yourself invisible, *your attacker is going to know that you are trying to run from them*. This means that they are going to get crafty in how they attempt to find you. Typically, this means sending people you would not suspect to try and gain information about you so that they can expose you to your attacker. New friends or acquaintances, mail delivery people, repairmen, personal investigators, and others may be incorporated into your attacker's attempt to locate you. If you are in a bad situation enough where you need to disappear, *you can trust that your attacker will not let up on attempting to find you easily.* You need to hide and stay hidden for the rest of your life to avoid being found by this person, as chances are, even if they stop looking, if they were to learn about you after, they would start up their pursuit once again.

# TECHNIQUES YOU NEED TO USE TO BECOME INVISIBLE

There are many things that you will need to do in order to completely disappear, so you have to prepare yourself mentally for a lot of work. Because there are likely many trails leading to you, you need to operate as quickly as possible. The following techniques have been listed in order of what is *most necessary to do right away,* to what you have a *little bit more time with accomplishing.* So, if you are trying to go under the radar completely, you want to follow these steps in order based on how they are laid out below.

## *Preparing To Leave*

Before you leave, you need to make sure that everything is ready for you to go.

➤ If you can, pay off any outstanding debt that you have so that you can completely cut ties with your banking companies to avoid being traced through your banks.

➤ You are also going to need to sell your properties or take your names out of any property agreements that you may have, as these can trace back to you as well if you are not careful.

➤ If you have enough time, inform your place of work and your children's school (if applicable) that you will be leaving so that they know that you will not be returning.

➤ It is also a good idea to have a stash of money saved up before you leave so that you can afford to pay for rent and your necessary bills for some time, as it may take you a while to be able to get a reliable place of employment once you are gone.

➤ Before you will be able to work again, you will need to have a new location and preferably a new legal name so that you cannot be tracked through your name.

➤ You will also need to opt for a new social security number so that you cannot be tracked through this information, either.

➤ The legal name change and change of personal identification documents, however, can be accomplished *after you are already gone and are physically safe* from any danger that may arise from your attacker.

What about your *family and friends*? If you have any family and friends who need to be notified, make sure that you tell them as well. Do not tell *anyone who you do not fully trust* about your plans, however, as this could lead to you being located by your attacker which is obviously not what you want. You need to make sure that the only people you tell are those who you can *absolutely trust* with the information that you are sharing with them. And even then, avoid giving any information such as where you will be located or what you are doing there with these individuals as any information they may have which could lead to you might be used to attempt to find you by your attacker. As a rule of thumb – the less other people know, the less they can tell either *accidentally* or *purposefully* to the person who might be trying to find you.

## Location

The first thing that you need to do is *change your location* since there is a good chance that virtually every trail associated with you right now will lead to where you are fairly quickly. By changing your primary location, every trail that presently exists will not be effective. While simply changing your location alone is not enough, this is the most important first step so that those who attempt to locate you are unable to get to you right away. This will give you immediate safety and more time to bury the rest of your trails.

*Leave Town*

➤ Since you are not going to want to be anywhere near where your original location, leaving your town is mandatory.

➤ If you have kids, pack up anything you need to bring with you into your vehicle and preferably leave at night when no one will be paying attention or expecting anything.

➤ If you can, go stay with a trusted family member or a close trusted friend in a different city until you are able to get your own place for you and your family to stay at more permanently.

➤ If you cannot stay with someone else and you need to stay in a hotel or a temporary rental at first, you want to make sure that you are not *using anything that could trace your location*. In other words, *do not pay with debit or credit in this location*. Instead, before you leave your home city, withdraw as much cash as you can and pay for everything in cash. You will not want to use your debit or credit cards anymore to avoid having your location traced.

*Renting or Leasing*

➤ Once you arrive in your new location, you need to make sure that you rent or lease and that you do not purchase a property. Purchasing a home can put your name permanently on the address, making it easier for you to be located by the person or people who are attempting to find you.

➤ If you can, rent or lease your property in *someone else's name* so that your address cannot be traced. Try to make sure that the people who are putting their name on your property know that they cannot disclose your address to anyone under any circumstances.

➤ Make sure that you rent a separate mailbox as well, preferably using someone else's name too, so that you can direct your mail to a separate address. This way, if anyone attempts to track you through your mail, they are not lead directly back to your property but instead, they are lead to your mailbox.

➤ Be cautious anytime you go to check your mail to be sure that no one is waiting for you or watching for you. If you can, rotate days and times that you go to your mailbox at so that it is never on a consistent, traceable schedule.

*Tying Up Loose Ends*

Typically when you leave a location, especially if you have children, you need to tie up some loose ends to make sure that a police report is not filed in an attempt to locate you or your children. Here are the steps:

➤ You will want to call your employer (if you have one) and inform them of your move and call your children's' school as well to inform them.

- Do not give away any information that may make you traceable in these phone calls, and when you make them, ensure that they are made from payphones that are far away from the place where you will be living more permanently.
- If possible, drive to a neighboring city and use a payphone so that your location is separate from the location where these individuals were contacted from.
- If you need to, create an excuse (work on it before your call) for why you had to leave unexpectedly and why you will not be back so that no one asks questions. You might say that a close family member fell ill unexpectedly and that you would be staying with them long-term so that you can take care of them, thus meaning you and your children will not be able to return any time soon.

## Personal Identity

You need to be extremely careful about your personal identity when it comes to disappearing because this is where most people will trip up and get caught almost immediately after fleeing a dangerous situation. Everything that could be connected to you needs to be hidden so that you are not able to be located once you have found a new safe location to go. You can do this by ensuring that no one or next to no one knows your new location, by destroying any garbage that may have your name on it, and by not using anything that could personally identify you such as your debit cards or your GPS tracking devices.

*Legal Name and Identification Documents*

➤ As soon as you can, get into a legal office and begin the process of changing your name and your social security number.

➤ Make sure that you are honest and clear about why this is happening, to protect your safety and the safety of your family so that the legal offices can support you in burying your trail as much as possible.

➤ It can take up to six months, if not longer, for legal changes like this to be processed so it is important that you are prepared to protect your identity by using family member's information or friend's information on legal agreements such as leases until your change is legal.

➤ Whenever possible, choose routes that will not result in you being personally identified by anyone who you are associated with. The fewer people who know about who you are and where you are from, the fewer chances you have of being located by the people who are trying to find you.

*Your Vehicle*

➤ Your vehicle can be an easy way for people to locate you as it has a VIN, license plate, and insurance that are all linked to your personal information.

➤ The best opportunity to hide is to sell your vehicle and purchase a second one in cash and then purchase your insurance in cash as well.

➤ If you can, get a trusted family member or a friend to put their name on the purchase and on the insurance until your legal name is changed so that you can transfer it back into your name. That way, you are not going to be associated with the new vehicle that you have purchased.

*Your Garbage or Identifying Documents*

➤ Your personal trash may contain information that could give away details about who you are and where you are located, so it is imperative that you are not putting any personal identification information in the trash either at your house or anywhere else.

➤ Any documents that have your name or other personal information on them should immediately be destroyed when you are ready to discard of them so that they cannot be read or traced.

➤ For example, if you receive a banking statement to your home even if it has your new legal name on it, destroy it so that no one can trace you through that piece of information. You should do this with anything, from envelopes with your name on it to notes sent back to you from your children's schools with their names on it. Anything with any form of identity should be burned to avoid it being turned into evidence or a paper trail to locate you and your family once you have chosen to disappear.

➤ Even if you go so far as to move to a new country, continue doing this just for an added layer of protection.

*Facial Recognition*

➤ As much as possible, you need to avoid being in any situation where you may be able to be visibly recognized by those around you so that you are not get caught when you are out in public or running general errands.

➤ If at all possible, change your physical appearance up enough so that people passing by would be less likely to identify you based on facial recognition. Changing your hairstyle and color, wearing different styled clothes, and even changing the way you wear your makeup and shape your eyebrows can all support you in changing your look.

➤ You can also wear accessories such as large sunglasses and hats to help cover up your face and any other identifiable features you may have.

➤ If you have tattoos or other unique aspects that make you easy to identify, you will need to cover these up when you go out in public to avoid being identified by these markers.

Aside from someone physically recognizing your face, you also need to avoid being on camera in any way at all.

➤ If you see someone filming or taking photographs, do your best to cover your face or avoid that camera to avoid being seen on film.

➤ If you are in a store and there are security cameras, keep your face pointed down or away from the cameras to avoid being caught on these tapes which may then be used by PIs or other investigators in an attempt to locate you. The less you and your children are seen on camera, the better.

## Children's Identity

Your children need to be protected as well, which means that you are going to need to take the proper action to change their identity and avoid having them found as well. Unfortunately, children may be more challenging to hide than you are because it is not as easy to change their appearances. However, you can opt for a different hairstyle and a different dressing style to attempt to throw people off from a distance or avoid them from being seen right away. You should also ensure that your children know how to protect their own identity so that when they are at school or at a friend's house, they are not being located.

*Protecting their Identity at School*

➤ At school, do your best to refrain from having your child called by their first name or their legal name so that they are less likely to be identified by those around them. If possible, choose a nickname for them and ensure that their teachers and friends call them by that nickname to avoid having them use their real name.

➤ If you are particularly concerned, such as if your children are equally at risk of being approached by your attacker, consider homeschooling them instead so that you can have a greater level of control over where they go and who they are surrounded by. This way, your children cannot be approached at school by people who may be trying to locate you or steal them back so that they can be returned to a dangerous situation.

➤ If you choose this option, please ensure that your child still has the opportunity to engage in extracurricular activities so that they are not being cut off from socializing altogether, that way they do not grow up feeling scared or isolated.

➤ Make sure that you are nearby or watching these extracurriculars and that you are paying for them in cash when you do. If possible, refrain from filling out any documents that name your children's legal names so that they are not being tracked by your attackers, either.

*Protecting their Identity in Social Circles*

➤ Again, chances are, you want to refrain from having too much disruption to your children's lifestyle as you do not want to traumatize them any more than your disappearance has likely already done. For that reason, you do not want to completely cut your children off from having a social life.

➤ However, you do need to be cautious to ensure that their social life is not somehow putting your family back on the radar. The best way to do this is to make sure that your children *do not have access to social media or the internet* – until they are old enough to understand the importance of protecting their own privacy and the privacy of your family.

➤ When they are old enough, make sure that you check in on their activities often so that you can monitor their behaviors and avoid them exposing your family through their online activities.

## Career

Once you get to your new location, you are going to need to begin making money so that you can earn a livable wage. After all, just because you are no longer traceable does not mean that living will be completely free or any cheaper than it was, to begin with. When you are trying to go off the radar completely, the best form of employment that you can take to is a *home-based career which can be done remotely and without ever telling anyone where you are located.* In fact, in most instances, you do not even have to give away your real name or any personally identifying information to the people who you are working with.

*Home Based Businesses That Work*

➤ Ideally, you want to get into a home-based business using a skill that you already have so that you can begin making money quickly. Places like Craigslist, Upwork, Fiverr, Kijiji, and other classifieds are a great opportunity to find work that you can do remotely.

➤ You can begin building your own business offering your services so that you can begin getting paid without getting located. Everyone's skills are going to vary, so you are going to need to determine which skills of yours are going to be the most profitable and start working towards earning an income using those skills.

➤ At first, you may need to establish a reputation for yourself which means that you may need to take on several odd jobs as you work toward building a name for yourself in your chosen area of business.

- For example, if you were a marketing agent in your career, you might start a small marketing firm from your computer and then take odd jobs such as landscaping work and moving jobs so that you can be paid in cash and start earning money right away.

- Once you begin to build a name for yourself in your chosen area, you will find that you are earning more income that way and you will not need to take as many odd jobs, but until then, you need to do whatever you can to earn an income and afford your cost of living.

- Avoid getting an *official job* at all costs, as the minute you apply for such a job, you need to input personal identification information such as banking information and your social security number which means that you will be traceable.

- If you have to get a job, see if you can get one under the table that pays in cash or checks and not direct deposit so that you are not required to give any personal information over to your employer on paper. This way, you can get paid reliably and without getting traced through your place of employment.

*Getting Paid for Your Work*

- When you get paid for the work you do, you should always seek to get paid through cash.

- If you are running an online business and getting paid online, make sure that you use a PayPal account or another online service like PayPal so that your money goes into a remote banking location.
- If you can, simply pay out of PayPal *for everything* that you are paying for. This way, you can attach a different name to your PayPal account and it is not able to be traced back to you.
- Once you have legally changed your name and social security number, you can open up a brand new bank account with your new legal name and social security number and begin depositing money into that account.
- However even then, avoid using the bank card provided to you and instead withdraw cash so that you are not able to be traced through your banking behaviors should anyone realize that you have changed your identification information.
- If you have checks or money orders that need to be mailed to you, always have them mailed to a PO box at the local post office and not to your house, to avoid being traced.

## *Internet*

The internet is a spot where you can quickly be located if you are not careful. This step is really important - *you should not bring any technological devices that you had in your old life when you disappear*. This is because these devices will all be linked to your personal information and hooked up to location services, which means that *you will be traceable*. Leave your phone, your iPads, your laptops, and everything else behind so that you are not able to be located the minute you turn these devices on and log in. If you need a phone to take with you, get a burner phone or a prepaid phone that cannot be connected to the internet so that you are not traceable.

*Location Services*

➤ Once you get to your new location, make sure that any devices you buy are paid for in cash and that your phones are always prepaid.

➤ Never log in with your old e-mails or passwords, as this will result in you immediately being traceable through your old accounts. Instead, create brand new accounts and ensure that these are never associated with your old ones.

➤ You should make sure that your children do the same if they are old enough to have the internet so that you can avoid having them being located by those who might be looking for you.

➤ If your children are not old enough to understand that they should not be trying to contact certain people or getting in contact with certain people online or through their phones, they should not have access to phones or the internet until they are old enough. That way, they are not accidentally exposing you and your family to your attacker and put you directly back on the radar through inappropriate online or mobile usage.

➢ When you do purchase new devices, it is also essential that you turn off the location services for *absolutely everything* and that you keep those services off for good.

➢ You should also refrain from using any GPS services that may require you to input personal information, such as Google GPS trackers which can be connected to your personal identity.

*Social Media*

➢ When it comes to social media, it can be very easy to get located if you are not careful. If possible, avoid using social media altogether to refrain from being connected with the people around you, as this can make it extremely easy for you to be located.

➢ If, however, you do choose to use social media, use it extremely wisely. Refrain from using any images that may show your face or your children's faces, as this will immediately offer the opportunity for people to identify you or your children and begin tracing you.

➢ As well, do not use your proper or legal names, as this makes it easier for people to locate you. Even if there are many people with your legal name, chances are, you are the only one who is directly connected to your social circle, meaning that it would be easy to determine whether or not that account was linked to you or someone else.

➤ On social media, keep your privacy settings as strict as possible and never include any information that could make you easy for someone to locate.

➤ Never connect your new city or neighborhood to your social media accounts, as even after you delete it, there is a chance that it could still be linked to your account somewhere on the internet which means that you will now be locatable.

➤ When creating your accounts, use fake emails so that they are not associated with your new emails, which will ensure that if anyone does find you and attempt to trace you through your social media, they will come up short.

➤ Never connect your phone number or other contact information to your social media account, aside from your fake email address. As well, never send this information through social media messages, email messages, or anywhere else online as this can be traced by anyone who may be trying to locate you as well.

*Online Banking*

➤ Any banking that you do should always be done *in person* to avoid having your location identified through your online banking activities.

➢ IP addresses and VPNs can quickly link people back to your location, help them identify which computer you are using, and ultimately result in you being traced.

## Banking and Legal Obligations

➢ As I mentioned in the beginning of this chapter, before you leave your original location, do your best to terminate any legal contracts or documents that may keep you obligated to someone or something in any way.

➢ Get your name taken off of any marital papers, property ownership documents, vehicle ownership documents, or anything else as much as possible.

➢ If you need to, transfer your assets into someone else's name so that they are no longer connected to you. This way, you do not necessarily have to give everything up but you are no longer legally associated with these things so your traceability is reduced.

➢ When you do open up a bank account and new legal or contractual obligations in the future, such as leases or electricity services, make sure that you either do so in someone else's name or that you have fully changed your legal name beforehand. This way, you are not able to be directly tracked through your name in association with any legal documents that you may have.

## Family and Friends

➤ In some cases, you may need to completely cut ties with your friends and family in order to protect yourself, and if applicable, your children from the person who is attempting to find you.

➤ In this case, make sure that you do not give anyone any information as to what you are doing as they may use this information against you, or this information may put them at risk of getting in trouble with anyone who is attempting to locate you.

➤ If you need to completely leave, make a clean break and refrain from ever contacting anyone again unless, for some reason, it becomes completely safe for you to do so.

➤ If you believe that you can continue having some contact with those that you love, make sure that your contact is minimal and that they are completely clear that they are not to tell anyone about where you or your family are.

➤ Do not invite your loved ones over to your place or give them your contact information as this will mean that they have access to information that other people may be trying to gain. Instead, you contact them from burner phones or pay phones any time you want to talk and you go to their homes and visit them if you are going to be visiting with anyone. They should know that any planned visits are not to be disclosed with anyone, under any circumstances, without your permission first. When you arrive, park away from where their home is so that you are not seen getting into and out of your car and make sure that no one is following you or watching you when you are going.

➤ As well, do not visit anyone who may be in your *old city or neighborhood* as this will put you directly in a danger zone. Instead, have these individuals meet you in a neutral location where you are unlikely to be seen or identified by anyone around you.

## *The Outside World*

When you are going completely under the radar, you never know who may be attempting to track you and provide your attackers with information regarding your whereabouts. You need to be extremely cautious with anyone who may be trying to get information about you, to avoid having information leaking through unexpected ways. UPS people, mail delivery individuals, and even home service repairmen can all be potential leaks so you need to be extremely cautious when you are allowing any of these people to have access to information of yours. Whenever possible, have all of your mail and packages delivered to a remote location or a trusted family member or friend who can give them to you at a later date.

- If you need a repairman to service your home, do not give them any personal information about who you are when they come and make sure that there are no personal identification factors readily available for them to observe.
- All of your mail, personal family pictures, and other identifiable documents should be hidden so that this individual cannot see anything associated with you or your family.
- You should also pay them in cash to ensure that they are not going to have access to your banking records or information through your payment method.
- If you need to pay by debit or credit, purchase a one-time use Visa with cash and pay them using that card so that they are not connected with your personal information.
- Should the service need to be signed for, either sign it using a different name or have a confidant over who can sign for you at the time.

Always be extremely cautious about who you give personal information to, and whenever possible, keep your personal information private or away from anyone who may be able to use it against you. The less anyone knows about who you are, the better. No one should be trusted when you are going completely under the radar, as anyone could be working for your attacker. You never know which route your attacker may attempt to go in order to locate you and make your move, so you always need to be thinking a few steps ahead of them.

## *Long-Term Outlook*

When you are looking for a complete disappearance, you need to realize that *every action* you take to disappear is going to need to *continue to be taken from the day you disappear forward*. You never know when your attacker may attempt to strike and even if they do stop looking for you if you were to become sloppy in hiding your tracks and they somehow happened upon your personal information, they may immediately begin their attempts once again. Once you have disappeared, you need to *stay disappeared* in order to protect yourself and your family from the dangers of your attackers for the rest of your lives.

This means that for the rest of your life, you should always be following the steps outlined in this chapter to ensure that you are not giving away any information that could lead to your identification and location. If and when you do make new friends in your new location, make sure that you are always very cautious about what you say to anyone or where you spend your time together as you never know who may be connected with your attacker and who may be innocent. If you do reach that point where you feel completely trust someone, you should still be extremely cautious about any information that you share with them as you do not want to accidentally open up to someone who could be working for your attacker.

# CONCLUSION

Now that you have completed *Watch Me Disappear*, I sincerely hope that you feel more confident about what needs to be addressed in order for you to protect yourself and your family to any degree that you need to.

Anonymity is important for anyone, but it is especially important for those who are trying to steer clear of the dangers that may be lurking in the shadows of their lives. If you have someone actively looking to cause harm to you or your family, simply staying clear of that individual by keeping your privacy settings on Facebook set to a "strict security" may not be enough. You need to ensure that *every aspect* of your life is hidden so that you are protected from the potential dangers of this person.

Needing to protect yourself and your family against attackers is not something that everyone will understand, so, unfortunately, you may have to burn many bridges and let go of a lot of aspects of your past life in order to reach the level of anonymity that you may need to stay safe. Sadly, the more anonymity you need, the more it has the capacity to wreak havoc on your mental health and on your life in general. The fear of your attacker lurking around any corner can be terrifying and it will be something that you may have to live with for the rest of your life depending on who your attacker is and how motivated they are to find you. Add to that the need to keep so many aspects of your life private or completely dissociate from who you were previously altogether in order to protect yourself and your family, and you can find yourself feeling extremely isolated, fearful, and shameful about you and your life. If you have children, you may also be feeling an intense level of regret and fear for their wellbeing and they will likely also be suffering, too. For that reason, you are going to need to make sure that you are spending as much time as possible *nurturing your mental health* and *taking care of your family* to avoid having intense traumatic repercussions from your need to hide.

Remember, if you need to completely disappear, you need to maintain that way of life *for the rest of your life*. You never know when your attacker may attempt to resurface and come back into your life to cause harm to you and your family. In fact, even in some cases of partial disappearances, you may need to be extremely cautious to avoid finding yourself crossing paths with your attacker once again. Like in my circumstance, I continue to ensure that my family's identity is protected and that the trails I have buried remain buried so that my paternal family does not attempt to locate me and harass me, my fiancé, and our child for money that they believe I owe them. I hope you will forgive me but it's exactly because of that I have changed some details about my biography for this book. If I was to allow any of these traceable factors to resurface, we would be at risk of being reproached and harassed for money. Since I do not know these people well, there is no way of knowing how far they might try and go if we were to come back into their radar, which leaves me fearful for my family's safety. You must always be cautious and stay cautious, as you do not want to undo all of the hard work that you have done to keep yourself safe from your family.

My last words of advice to you – once you are done reading this book, make sure that you do follow at least the *basic steps* to protect your anonymity on the internet. You may not want to disappear completely, but keeping your family safety at a high level is never a bad idea. And if you do suspect that someone is tracking you or planning something evil for you, there is enough advice in this book what can you do to protect yourself and your family to a better degree.

Before we part our ways – if you felt that **Watch Me Disappear** has supported you in understanding how to reach the extent of anonymity that you need, it would be fantastic if you could express your opinion on Amazon. It may help lead other people to the information that they need to protect themselves and their families as well.

Thank you and stay safe!

# PRACTICAL
# BONUS

The following are resources that you can use to help you protect your anonymity. I hope that these can further assist you on your goals to protect you and your family.

- **Tor Browser**: This anonymous browser application allows you to browse online and completely protects your privacy. Anytime you use Tor Browser, your information will be bounced through encryption programs to ensure that your IP address, location, and other traceable information are all hidden and dissociated from you and your actual location. https://www.torproject.org/download/

- **Use a *kill-all* account service**: There are many online services which offer to "clean your online presence". While none of them offers 100% effectiveness, it is still a good starting point when it comes to cleaning your digital footprint.
https://www.deseat.me
https://www.accountkiller.com
https://abine.com/deleteme

- **Hot Spot Shield**: This app will allow you to encrypt and protect your cloud storage so that anything you store in the cloud cannot be accessed by people who may be trying to hack your account or track you online. https://www.hotspotshield.com

- **VPNs**: Your VPN (*virtual private network*) connects you to your internet services. Use an anonymous VPN by going to a platform like Anonabox to get a private VPN so that you are not traceable. https://www.anonabox.com

- **Burner Accounts**: Create a series of fake emails that you can use with online platforms so that if you are ever traced through one of them, you can delete that email and continue using a different email. If you ever suspect that you have been tracked, immediately stop using that email. Make sure none of the emails are connected to each other or to your phone number. https://temp-mail.org/en/ https://maildrop.cc/

- **Go Incognito**: In almost all modern browsers there is a built-in "Private" or "Incognito" mode. This mode prevents your browser / online services which you use from collecting and storing basic identifiable information (such as login, password, your previous browsing sessions etc). While this is not a guarantee of complete online privacy, it's a good idea to use this browsing mode as *default*.

- **Use Prepaid Credit Cards**: If you need to buy something online or where cash is not accepted, purchase a prepaid credit card with cash and use that to pay for your product or services. Have them delivered to a remote mailbox so that they are not able to be traced directly back to you. Use a fake name on the package if you can or no name at all to avoid being identified through your mail.

- **Consider Moving to Europe**: Europe values your privacy and will support you in staying hidden. Their latest GDPR will keep you protected both online and offline.

CPSIA information can be obtained
at www.ICGtesting.com
Printed in the USA
LVHW041459121020
668590LV00002B/625